CRAP CARS

RICHARD PORTER

BBC
BOOKS

Published by BBC Books, BBC Worldwide Ltd,
Woodlands, 80 Wood Lane, London W12 0TT

ISBN 978 0 563 52210 2

Commissioning Editor: Ben Dunn
Project Editor: Sarah Emsley
Designer: Nick Fell
Picture Researcher: Giles Chapman
Copy-editor: Barnaby Harsent
Production Controller: Christopher Tinker

Origination by Butler & Tanner Ltd
Printed and bound in Singapore by Tien Wah Press
13 15 17 19 20 18 16 14 12

CONTENTS

50 LANCIA MONTE CARLO

Let's start with a car that wasn't really that crap at all. It was quite quick, largely nice to drive and invigorating in that Italian way that immediately makes you want to dress better and wear sunglasses. There was just one problem. Under anything more than light braking the front wheels would lock and the car would slide terrifyingly towards the nearest unyielding roadside object. The problem was serious. So serious that Lancia actually stopped selling the Monte Carlo for more than a year while they sought a solution. The glitch was swiftly traced to that bit of modern cars that amplifies brake effort from the pedal to the wheels – the servo. And after months of head-scratching Lancia had a fix. They unplugged it. Brilliant.

49
PORSCHE 924

A low performance Porsche? Isn't that as pointless as explaining income tax to a horse? Yep. The wet-lettuce 924's life started when Volkswagen asked Porsche to design a coupe for them. Then, having emptied out all their pockets, rifled through their spare jacket and pulled all the cushions off the sofa, VW realised they didn't have the cash to pay for it and beat a red-faced retreat. However, since the car was pretty much ready, Porsche simply slapped their own badge on it and put it on sale without even changing the VW engine for one of their own. Which was an error when you discovered which VW the engine came from – the LT van. Doh! Unsurprisingly, while it might have worked perfectly well in something square and white and filled with ladders, in a pointy-fronted coupe it was utterly pathetic. A while later Porsche pulled up their lederhosen, fitted one of their own engines and turned it into the 944, which was rather good.

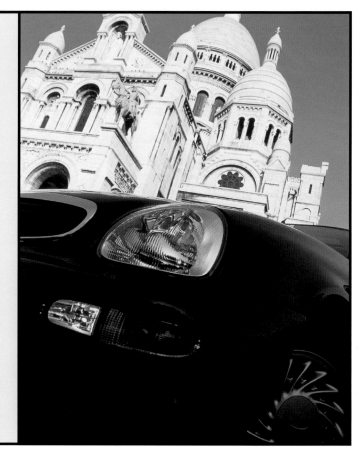

48 FORD SCORPIO

Executive cars are meant to convey a combination of taste, affluence and discretion. The Scorpio did none of these. On the other hand, it was fantastically good at scaring children.

47 CADILLAC STS

When it came to finding chunky jewellery and pungent cigars, the rise of the 'Everything For A Pound' shop meant that the fat, northern nightclub owner was spoilt for choice. But getting a car to fit their tubby, sweaty frames was trickier. That is until Vauxhall generously stepped into the breach by importing this chintzy horror from America. The nasty disco proprietor might have found the exterior a bit low key, but the interior more than compensated, what with its greasy plastics, crumpled leather and funny brown trim that was a loose approximation of 'wood'. Suddenly the boss of 'Chinos' or 'Shaggers' could enjoy all the clammy and charmless tack of their business premises in one conspicuously vulgar package. Except, as it happened, they weren't interested. And nor was anyone else – British STS sales could be counted on the sovereign-ring-clad fingers of one hand. Apparently even northern nightclub owners have some taste.

46 RENAULT SAFRANE

Small cars, shrugging and garlicky food. These are things the French are good at. But asking them to make a decent big car is like asking them to stop flirting with your girlfriend or to join in with your war. It's not going to happen. But that doesn't stop them, hence the feeble effort you see here. As if anyone in their right mind would have thought, 'Oooh, shall I have one of those nice Audis or shall I flush a large amount of cash down the lavatory by picking up one of those crap new Renaults?' Erm… Frankly, the only reason the Safrane ever existed in the first place was to give French civil servants something reasonably comfortable in which to dash across Paris in time to have another affair.

45 JAGUAR XJ40

When the XJ40 was announced it was tarted about as a 'clean-sheet design'. Actually sometime in the 1970s Jaguar had taken that 'clean sheet', written on it everything that people loved about their cars – curvy styling, traditional interiors, strong performance – and then screwed it up and thrown it into the sea. So we ended up with this box-fronted horror with its abysmal amusement-arcade dashboard and, in basic 2.9-litre form, the rampant acceleration of a slug in a bag. However, while Jag may have bragged that everything about the XJ40 was brand new, they managed to hang on to some features from their old cars, chiefly the one that made random bits fall off or stop working properly. Oh, and while the front of the car was craggy and square, the back end was saggy and curved, which, it later emerged, may have been accidental. Allegedly, Jag had carved the design out of clay and sent it away to be turned into real metal, except during its journey the clay model melted, giving the finished article a slack-arsed appearance that no one remembered to fix. Durrr.

44 FORD ESCORT MKIV

During the 1980s Ford's primary aim wasn't making cars, it was making money. And this was the grimmest moment of its penny-pinching, bottom-line-enhancing ways. Every single part of the Escort felt like the accountants had examined it, jabbed some numbers into a calculator, reduced the cost by 15 per cent, and then lopped another quid off it. The result was a car of almost unmatched dismalness. Imagine picking a nice grey November day to sit in the shallow water of the River Humber eating lard sandwiches. Driving the Escort delivered about that amount of joy. Minus 15 per cent.

43 YUGO SANA

Unbreakable rules of car buying, number 57: never spend your money on something that sounds like a new type of sanitary towel.

42
MITSUBISHI 3000GT

If you or I sat down and drew a smirking girl sitting in front of a lake it probably wouldn't be quite as good as the Mona Lisa. So when Mitsubishi, hitherto a maker of rugged 4x4s and tedious saloons, set out to make a proper sports car it was pretty unlikely to be a Japanese Porsche. More likely it would be fat and inept and made by people who erroneously assumed that the way to make a car good was to lather it with a skipful of the sort of useless technology more commonly found in those supplements that fall out of Sunday papers. And indeed that's what it was. The 3000GT may have been quick but it was about as sporty as playing darts.

41 ROVER 800

The 800 marked Rover's closest cooperation to date with its Far-Eastern ally, Honda. The idea was brilliant – the Japanese would bring the build quality, the reliability and the precision engineering, and the British would garnish it with their talent for suspension tuning and classic, tasteful design. What could possibly go wrong? Apart from Rover completely ignoring Honda's suggestions on, say, how to make the doors fit properly, blithely ploughing on with their own ideas, and not only delaying the whole project but also managing to bugger up the entire car. Honda finished their version of the 800 months ahead of Rover simply because they didn't waste time re-inventing things to make them crappier. Called the Legend, it didn't look as nice or drive as well as its Rover sister, but the 800 is in this book and the Legend isn't for one very good reason: you can flaunt all the swishier styling and smarter chassis settings you want, but if the bootlid doesn't fit properly and the dashboard turns green in strong sunlight it doesn't matter – your car is crap.

40 VOLVO 340

Before they got all sexed up in the nineties, Volvo was synonymous with estate cars that were good for one thing – carrying stuff. All the 340 could carry was the shame of being the runt of the family, a wheezy hatchback that appealed largely to senile pensioners who were too well-heeled to drive a Metro. High spot of the 340's glitteringly shit career was an ill-advised ad campaign that dared to suggest that it cornered 'like a Porsche', purely because, like some of Germany's finest sports cars, the Volvo carried its gearbox at the back. But then Southend is on the coast but that doesn't make it in any way 'like the South of France'. Weirdly, this Volvo wasn't even Swedish – it was designed and built in Holland. What were they schmoking?

39 DELOREAN DMC-12

The DMC-12 was the baby of John Z Delorean, a silver-haired cowboy figure who spent the sixties inventing tasty cars for General Motors in Detroit. That's the kind of cool stuff you get to do when your middle name starts with a Z. The trouble started when John Z got bored with working for The Man and decided to create his own 'ethical' sports car. Originally those ethics revolved around environmental concern, although the whole project soon became mired in the rather less ethical business of wringing big sacks of cash out of the British government. Some of the money was used to set up a brand new factory in Belfast; Lotus took the rest in return for developing the car itself. And the end result looked pretty stunning, at least until that stainless steel body got covered in fingerprints and bird poo. It sounded pretty meaty too, what with a 2.8-litre V6 at the back. Sadly its performance was actually weaker than a baby deer, and sales were dismal, falling rapidly to nought when John Z got embroiled in a doomed cocaine deal, and had to shut his car factory forever. The car did rise again as the star of *Back To The Future*, although even in 1955 they'd probably have noticed it was rubbish.

38 VAUXHALL BELMONT

Mmm, all the joyless suffocation of being trapped inside the lobby of a nursing home … in a car. The mid-eighties Vauxhall Astra was kind of radical in its day, what with that smooth teardrop shape and the option of a digital speedometer. Rather too radical for the kind of senile, dot-brained, *Daily Express* reading coot who might have bought the old model and used it to putter to the post office at precisely 27 mph. Fortunately Vauxhall had the answer with this, the Belmont. The cute snub-nosed front of the Astra remained but it was more than offset by the massive and crashingly traditional saloon boot, artlessly welded to the back. It was like forcing Cameron Diaz to appear in every scene of her next movie wearing an Australian backpacker's rucksack. So that was the looks utterly ruined, and the driving experience was suitably pedestrian to match. But the real joy of the Belmont was its miserable, soulless interior, especially in the top-of-the-tree CD model, which sported a sticky velour covering for almost every interior surface up to and including the rear parcel shelf. The only thing missing was a walking-stick holder.

37 TRIUMPH TR7

Legend has it that Italian car-design genius Giorgetto Giugiaro first encountered the TR7 on a motor-show stand. He stood for a moment, staring at the weird creases up the flank, wandered halfway around the car and declared, 'My God, they've done it to the other side too'. No-one knows if this story is true but it seems unlikely, not least because a more plausible reaction would have been 'My God, it's completely shit!' The TR7's unpleasant turret roof came from fears that the Americans were about to introduce stiff requirements for roll-over protection that would kill traditional British roadsters. Fair enough, but what happened at Triumph? Did they misread the rules and think the roof had to be so ugly that in the event of a roll the ground would actually attempt to repel it? Still, although it had a roof and looked terrible, the TR7 did at least cling on to some other 'traditional' British roadster qualities. That's why it was slow, wheezy and as solidly assembled as a Cadbury Flake.

36 ROLLS-ROYCE CARMARGUE

See, even very rich people like a joke every now and again.

35 TALBOT TAGORA

Talbot Tagora – it sort of sounds like the name of someone who anchors a late-night current affairs show on American TV. So it's a bit disappointing to discover that, rather than being a slick news monkey with big hair and a Tango complexion, the Tagora is actually an utterly dismal executive car of such extraordinary squareness that it appears to have been designed on an Etch-a-Sketch. The biggest problem with this car is that large parts of it were designed in France, which pretty much amounts to a kiss of death for any large car. And even by the epically unsuccessful standards of the average French big car, the Tagora was a glorious failure, lasting for just three years before Talbot's new owners Peugeot stopped making it. And then they killed the entire company, just to be on the safe side.

34 SUZUKI WAGON R

Misery can take many forms. Living for an entire month on margarine, for example, or boarding a London to Sydney flight and discovering that you've been given a seat next to Timmy Mallett. But there are very few things that could top the sheer deflating misery of having to drive one of these. There are dead things that offer more acceleration than the Wagon R and, while the spec sheet may have claimed that Suzuki had fitted it with something called 'suspension', there was no actual evidence that anything as yielding and comfortable as a 'spring' had ever been installed between the wheels and the body. But the real horror of the Wagon R was its amusing appearance. Perhaps even Suzuki was surprised to learn that Victorian villains, Coldstream Guards and members of the High Church just waiting for a car they can wear their hat in, do not constitute a 'demographic'.

33 **VOLVO 262C**

One of the greatest things about mankind is our constantly enquiring minds that lead us to conquer continents, explore space and invent a way to electrically clip your nose and ear hair. But there are some questions that don't need answering. Questions such as, 'I wonder if I could drop this glockenspiel on my own head?', 'What would happen if I lived entirely on crisps?' and, worst of all, 'What would happen if you sliced the roof off an otherwise sensible Volvo saloon and replaced it with what appears to be the top of a 1970s American pimp mobile?' Well here's your answer – it would look ridiculous. But that didn't stop them making it. Doh!

32 SUBARU XT

Four-wheel drive is, by and large, a good thing. In off-roaders it's often switched on all the time, to haul you out of muddy ruts. In sports cars it only works when you need it, to improve grip in slippery corners. But what about the Subaru XT? Plainly this wasn't an off-roader but neither, despite the ever-so-pointy coupe styling, was it really a sports car. So what sort of four-wheel drive system would it have? Permanent? Part-time? Or one that worked when you switched on the windscreen wipers? Sadly, it was the third one. There was more mentalness in the steering wheel – which was bizarrely asymmetrical, with an L-shaped middle – and the gear stick – which was plainly meant to look like a jet fighter's joystick though it actually resembled a big cock. But nothing, not even getting Magnus Pike to travel everywhere with you on the back seat, could match the strangeness of that four-wheel drive arrangement which, just to remind you, was linked to the windscreen wipers. Ummm…

31 NISSAN SUNNY COUPE

So what happened here then? Was the bloke who could draw curves out of the office that day? Or was this some sort of tribute to the great Japanese traditions of origami, in which case why didn't they go the whole hog and make the wheels square too? Frankly it couldn't have made it any more horrible to drive. You might have thought 'coupe' meant something fast and sporty. You would be terribly, terribly wrong. This was based on the Sunny hatchback, a car of such soul-destroying dullness that even nipping around the corner for a bottle of milk and a paper could comprehensively erase your will to live. Still, in the case of the coupe, at least if you were driving you didn't have to look at the outside.

30 SKODA ESTELLE

In the 1980s there was a pretty established way to build an engine. You made the cylinder block out of iron -– heavy, strong, perfect for containing the small explosions that make an engine go – and topped it with a cylinder head made of aluminium – light, precise, perfect for containing the fiddly system of valves and camshafts that allow an engine to breathe. Unless you were Skoda. Then you got it completely the wrong way round, made the head out of clunky iron and the block out of light aluminium. Then, for good measure, you put that engine in the wrong place – at the back – where it could make a right old cock-up of the handling. Perhaps they were holding the plans upside down.

29 RENAULT 9

Terrifyingly, this won European Car of the Year back in 1982, which just goes to show that if people can't agree on the candidate they like, the winner will be the one that no-one likes at all. This was Renault's attempt to sell more cars by ruthlessly erasing all style and character from them. The 9 wasn't just boring to look at, driving it was so oppressively dull and forgettable that unless you parked it right outside the front door there was a very real chance that you'd get up in the morning and catch the bus to work before wondering why it was you'd found the journey unusually enjoyable for once.

28 MASERATI BITURBO

Mmm, Maserati. Doesn't the very mention of its name make you think of swishing across Europe in a cool sixties coupe, en route to a rendezvous in a Monte Carlo casino where your winning ways will seduce a girl who looks like Audrey Hepburn before leaving arm-in-arm, perhaps pausing to punch a man in a fez. And then you see this – the Biturbo. Old Maseratis were called cool and exotic things like Mistral, Khamsin and Kyalami, so what sort of tediously functional name was that? Also, Maseratis were meant to be ruthlessly rakish sex wedges – who wants to swish through France in something that looks like a child's drawing of a car? Not that you'd make it much beyond Calais before it probably broke down. Which I suppose would at least spare you the embarrassment of arriving in Monaco in a really shit Maserati.

27 DAIHATSU MOVE

You have a choice. You can a) drive around in one of these or b) have a rusty nail banged into your head. I'll get the hammer…

26 ALFA ROMEO ARNA

Some time around the dawn of the 1980s Alfa needed a new entry-level model. At the same time Nissan wanted a car they could build in someone else's European factory, thereby dodging a 'gentlemen's agreement' that limited the number of vehicles that could be imported into the EEC from Japanese factories. The two companies decided to collaborate. The way you would have done this was simple. God, it was simple. A child could have worked it out. In fact, a child would have found it insultingly straightforward and given it to their dog, who would still have cracked it in about five minutes flat. You'd get the Italians, with their rich heritage of sculptural beauty and their ability to imbue mere mechanical things with a heart and a personality that makes your soul sing, to sort out the looks and the chassis. And you'd ask the Japanese, with their meticulous attention to detail and their ability to make even the cheapest, most mundane object with precision and everlasting quality, to sort out the functional aspects of actually getting the thing made. So what did Alfa and Nissan do? The exact opposite. Bravo!

25
HYUNDAI PONY

Great car companies usually rise out of one man's struggle against the odds to craft the seminal cars that will define the passion and joy of the company that bears his name. Hyundai was not one of those companies. It was an industrial conglomerate that made stuff like ships and railways, until one day it had the bright idea of branching into cars. The result was never going to be a Porsche or a Ferrari. Or indeed very good. In fact it was a miserable turd of a car whose only saving grace was that it was cheap. That and its tendency to go rusty, which at least gave you an excuse to have it crushed.

24 FIAT STRADA

During the 1970s Fiat did a pretty good impression of British Leyland, but with more coffee and a wider array of animated hand gestures. Same inability to make stuff work properly, same belief that if a car was going to go rusty it might as well start before it had even left the factory, same workforce that regularly renounced making anything in favour of standing around outside the factory demanding softer loo roll or something. So imagine Fiat's jealousy when they saw the Austin Allegro. The British had really stolen a march when it came to making a piggy-eyed, unreliable, laughing stock of a family car. Then the Italians launched the Strada. Checkmate. This car is best remembered for some cunning adverts that showcased Fiat's swishy new automated factory seamlessly bolting cars together above the tag line 'Handbuilt by robots'. Then you saw an actual Strada, complete with panel gaps you could slide a briefcase through, and you realized that Fiat had foolishly bought a batch of robots that were as sloppy and random as the workforce they were meant to replace. But with slightly fewer coffee breaks.

23
SUBARU JUSTY

If you locked someone in a room with a Justy for two weeks and then, on their release, asked them to sketch it, they'd draw a blank. That's how dull it was, and the interior was even more miserable, to the stage where you'd really only get inside if forced to at knife point. Worst of all, there was that foolishly weird name that just encouraged car journalists to make bloody puns about it. There's no way this car could ever be Justy-fied. Oh … damn.

22 AUSTIN MAESTRO

On paper the Maestro seemed like a good idea. Much like, say, ironing your clothes while still wearing them might seem like a good idea. Trying to make a spacious, economical and thoroughly sensible family hatchback was fair enough, but for one thing – the Maestro was designed by British Leyland. On early examples the panels were fitted so approximately there was a good chance you could get into the car without actually opening any of the doors and, worse still, it was misguidedly loaded with high technology in a vain attempt to make it seem modern. Given that Laurel and Hardy could have made a better job of screwing everything together, the last thing you'd want to do is make things unnecessarily complicated. The plastic bumpers cracked in cold weather, the electronic engine control had some very strange ideas about what sort of idle speed you might like, and the voice synthesizer that was meant to identify problems would issue hysterical warnings about things that weren't even faulty. Although given the general state of the Maestro you could probably consider this a pre-emptive strike.

21 TOYOTA SPACE CRUISER

Now on the surface you might think this was quite exciting. Not to look at, obviously, unless for no apparent reason you'd decided to read this book having first rubbed Tabasco sauce into your eyes. But the name seems somehow filled with excitingly futuristic promise. Space Cruiser. It sounds like something out of *Star Wars*. Unfortunately the actual car wasn't. Well, not unless everything had gone terribly wrong in a galaxy far, far away and interplanetary travellers were reduced to scuttling about in what amounted to an abysmal van that had been crudely converted into a poor approximation of a proper car simply by nailing some seats in the back, cutting windows in the side and spraying the whole thing in a nauseating two-tone paint scheme. Luke Skywalker may have been gutted to discover that Darth Vadar was his dad, but he'd have been really pissed off if he then learnt that the family car was one of these.

20 FIAT 126

The Fiat 500 was the car that mobilized Italy. It was cheap, it looked cute and it was so simple that legend has it only four mechanical bits could ever go wrong with it – largely because there were only four mechanical bits on it in the first place. But when Fiat decided to replace the 500 they got carried away trying to make it bigger and more sophisticated. The result was the 126, a nasty little motorized box with an engine that managed to be frenetic but ineffectual, like a hamster pushing a filing cabinet. The 126's defining moment came when Fiat invented a 'special edition' model. Usually such versions are called faintly exotic things like 'Tango' or 'Esplanade'. Alas, this version was painted a sort of unsettling poo colour and it was called the Fiat 126 … 'Brown'.

70

DAIHATSU
APPLAUSE

19 DAIHATSU APPLAUSE

Great car names tend to ripple with muscular promise or the rich scented suggestion of something tantalizingly exotic. Mustang, Cobra, Khamsin, that sort of thing. But 'Applause'? Um, no. What in the name of all that's holy is that meant to say about you? 'Yes, I drive an Applause…' It's not exactly the sort of idle nightclub boast that's going to lead you to a hotel suite with five members of the Danish Ladies' Beach Volleyball Team, two jars of honey and a trampoline. Why on earth would you want to saddle your new car with the hint of that limp-wristed clattering you get from the boundaries of a village cricket match? Were they in a rush and this was the first word they alighted on in the dictionary? Or was it an attempt to tell the world that this was a dismal piece of tinny, third-division junk with the kind of ghastly two-tone paint job that can only have been applied by someone who thought the basic design just wasn't abysmal enough? In which case, job done.

18 FERRARI 400

There are lost tribes in the Amazon Basin who could tell you that the two things you can expect from any Ferrari are performance and beauty. Shame, then, that Ferrari themselves completely forgot these facts before designing this minger. With a whopping great 4.8-litre engine up front you might vainly hope that this car would be quick but, since most 400s came with an automatic gearbox, the only thing it did quickly was slurp petrol into 12 hungry cylinders. Couple this with a galumphing chassis and disturbingly feeble brakes and you had a real recipe for misery. Which, in any other Ferrari would have been a great excuse to park it outside and spend your time staring at its trouser-dampening beauty. But not with this abject exercise in large-scale origami. A sobering reminder that the work-experience boy is there to make coffee, not design a car.

17 AUSTIN AMBASSADOR

Time for some shocking news: the Austin Princess was not a crap car. It looked almost futuristic, it had very clever suspension to give an exceptionally smooth ride and this was complemented by a spacious interior with fantastically comfortable seats. After the Allegro and the Marina and all the other slop that drizzled out of BL in the 1970s, this was a rare goal that wasn't punted into the back of their own net. For a company that had turned seizing defeat from the jaws of victory into an Olympic sport, clearly this would not do. So, a few years later, they turned the Princess into the Ambassador, a process that essentially involved combing through the car, identifying all the good bits, and then throwing them away. It looked worse, it was hopelessly slow and the interior was so grim that you'd only want to get inside if it was raining. The one thing that was notably improved was the appearance of a proper hatchback. Woo! Hold the front page. Otherwise the Ambassador was so hopeless that legend has it the boss of Leyland in Italy rang the factory and begged them not to send him any, possibly with the words 'Ambassador you are spoiling us…' Then again, probably not.

16 YUGO 45

As if years of in-fighting wasn't painful enough for the peoples of the former Yugoslavia, they also had to put up with this flaky little griefbox. The basics came from Fiat who, after off-loading designs to the Russians and the Poles, were making quite a nice business out of flogging tat to the other side of the Iron Curtain, but the Yugoslavs managed to add their own layer of ineptitude to the basic recipe. Hence the shabby styling, to which the British importers felt compelled to add a series of garish stickers, spotlights and, in some vomitous cases, a really cack bodykit, as if you wanted to draw attention to your cheapskatedness and complete lack of car-buying sense. There were also coughing engines, approximate build quality and dashboards made from the kind of plastics more usually found containing Tic Tacs. Still, when Yugoslavia descended into full blown war, at least someone had the presence of mind to bomb the factory.

15 DATSUN SUNNY 120Y

In the 1970s the Japanese were still getting the hang of making cars. They'd cracked reliability pretty quickly but some things still eluded them. Rust-proofing, for example. Specifically, working out that cars would probably last longer if you didn't build them from the sort of metal usually found wrapped around a stick of chewing gum. So, the 120Y's engine may have hummed on until the end of time, but the bodywork would have long since dissolved around it. It also handled like a shopping trolley full of logs and wore the weirdest wheel trims in the known world, apparently inspired by the containers you normally get steak and kidney pies in.

14 ASTON MARTIN LAGONDA

In the mid-seventies Aston Martin was in trouble. People didn't want to spend money on lavish, fuel-snorting British sports cars and the company was broke. So, what would you do next: a) hammer crooked bits of wood over the windows, keep upper lip twitchingly stiff, remember that the company has survived worse; or b) take a massive gun, point directly at foot, pull trigger? Aston picked the second option. They decided that the best way to face a crisis was to go completely mental and invent a massive luxury saloon that looked like it had fallen from space and came packed with zany technology like digital instruments and touch-sensitive buttons instead of a gear lever – neither of which had even the faintest chance of ever working properly. Hence, throughout its life the Lagonda was only popular in the Middle East, where they had lots of money to keep up with its terrifying appetite for petrol and lots of spare desert in which to abandon it when it broke down again.

13 SUZUKI SJ

For no good reason the SJ was often used as a hire car in the kind of 'fun' Mediterranean holiday resorts where 'fun' holiday companies organise 'fun' activities like the reps' cabaret or an organized vomiting festival. Which is strange, because the SJ itself was less 'fun' than being birched.

12 **FSO POLONEZ**

Mmm, a delicious blend of finely minced lean beef and Italian sausage wrapped in a smooth sauce of tomato, red wine and oregano. No, wait, that's bolognese. What we have here is a vomitous blend of crappy old bits that Fiat didn't want, ineptly stewed with some crappy new bits of FSO's own invention, the whole lot wrapped in an unpleasant and lumpy body and badly thrown together in a Polish factory to a standard that made a Shredded Wheat look sturdy. The Polonez also suffered the indignity of being at least as rubbish as a Skoda or a Lada without being notorious enough to provide annoying eighties comedians with the material for half their act. Which made it something even worse – a joke you have to explain.

11 SEAT MARBELLA

The Fiat Panda was a decent little car in a basic sort of way. However, after a few years Fiat realized that selling something based on technology that Neolithic man would have considered passé just wasn't on, and they redesigned the suspension before adding some brand new, up-to-date engines. They could afford to do this because around the same time they cunningly flogged the crappy old bits to Seat, who carried on making the original Panda, prehistoric technology and all, saddled with the none-more-cheesy Marbella badge. Perhaps in an attempt to stop buyers noticing that their 'new' car was less sophisticated than a potato, Seat smothered the bottom half of the bodywork with thick plastic cladding that just made it look like a bumper car, and made a similarly feeble effort to posh up the interior. The whole thing was less convincing than a baboon in lipstick pretending to be an air hostess.

MGB

For reasons that no-one can quite remember, the MGB is the darling of the classic-car scene. Which is odd because it's also quite spectacularly rubbish. For one thing, it's loosely based on the chassis of the Austin Cambridge, a 1950s saloon that used technology so old fashioned it gets several mentions in the Bible. Secondly, the MG wasn't the only thing to be built around the Cambridge chassis. It was also used as the basis for the Leyland Sherpa. Which is a van. So driving an MGB is essentially admitting that you've wasted your money on a leakier, noisier, less comfortable and far less handy version of something plumbers used to drive. In fact, there are only two things worse than actually driving an MGB: having to spend time with MGB owners in the back room of some country pub as they brag about how they spent 27 years re-chroming their bumpers or stripping down the entire gearbox using only their teeth; or having your face pushed into a lawnmower. Actually come to think of it, the lawnmower option suddenly sounds quite nice.

TRABANT

When the Berlin Wall came down, news reports claimed that East Germans 'flooded' over the former border. Not if they were driving Trabants they didn't. 'Farted' would have been more appropriate. What do you expect from a car powered by an engine so lame even the people who make electric carving knives would have deemed it feeble. Although, in fairness, the engine was jostling at the front of the pack to be voted the most utterly rubbish part of the car, with strong competition from the body, which was made of cardboard, and an interior that was so bleak even the Stasi would have considered more than half an hour in there as 'a bit cruel'. Before the old borders were broken down, us in the West thought we knew how harsh life was behind the Iron Curtain. Then we saw the Trabant. Oh, the humanity.

RELIANT ROBIN

The Reliant Robin holds the lap record at the famous Le Mans circuit in France. It was also the favoured transport of David Niven, Jack Nicholson and King Juan Carlos of Spain, and has been depicted on high-value postage stamps in Sweden, New Zealand and the People's Republic of the Congo. In Japan the highest honour a samurai can receive is to be given an R-reg Reliant Robin fitted with the desirable AM radio option, while in some parts of Kenya it is believed that anyone who drives a Robin is blessed with great fertility and sexual magnetism. Ah, hang on, I was thinking of something else. The Robin is an unloved pile of shit. Sorry.

BOND BUG

Cheese. Nice enough on toast, an utterly stupid thing to use as the inspiration for car design. But that's what appears to have happened here, especially since they only sold it in orange. As it turned out, the looks were but a fart in a hurricane compared to the way it drove. You could have guessed as much when you noticed that the Bug only had three wheels, pretty much a guarantee of weapons-grade rubbishness in any car. Trouble was, since the little Bond weighed slightly less than a pair of shoes, introducing a person into the equation did funny things to the handling, to the point where taking a left-hand bend at anything more than retired tortoise pace would make it fall over. Some owners tried to counter this by putting bricks on the passenger seat, which was fine until you gave someone a lift and were forced to relegate those bricks to the 'boot' behind you. At which point the front wheel would lift off the ground. Brilliant. Frankly, you'd have been better off trying to drive around in an actual piece of cheese. At least fewer people would have laughed at you.

NISSAN SERENA

6

Amazingly the name wasn't the worst thing about this car. No, that would be the almost complete lack of anything resembling 'performance'. For many years the diesel version could claim to be the slowest accelerating car in Britain, its 0-60 time being measurable in months. In fact the front wheel could pass over a patch of ground, a flower could seed, grow and give up its sweet nectar to bees with plenty of time to spare before the rear wheel would crush it to the floor. The problem was compounded when you remember that this was a people carrier, like the very thing it needed was the weight of extra bodies to erase what little forward motion it could offer. Nowadays Serenas seem to be the exclusive preserve of rubbish minicabbers. If one turns up outside your house you'd better not be in a hurry.

LADA RIVA

This is the real reason the Russians had it tough under Communist rule. You'd pay the equivalent of a million years' wages, lose your place in the meat queue and only get to use the village bath plug during years with a four in them, and in return you got one of these. A cheap and incompetent remix of a sixties Fiat, which offered grimness of such miserable depth that it must have made you long for some sort of respite. A visit from the KGB Torture and Poison Division perhaps.

MORRIS MARINA

Some time in the late 1960s, someone at BMC or British Leyland or whatever it was called that week noticed that the Ford Cortina was rather successful and decided to build a rival. Since the Cortina was a simple machine, this hot new competitor would be resolutely low tech too. Thing is, there's low tech and there's basing a car on the Morris Minor, which was in turn based on something Noah found in his shed. Star turn in this festival of mediocrity was the Marina's cornering ability. Or rather, its complete lack of it. This car took corners with all the sure-footed competence of a child on roller skates. Later in life they gave it a facelift and renamed it the Ital, thus proving beyond doubt that you really can't polish a turd.

SUZUKI X90

Why do people buy 4x4s? Because they look rugged and are packed with the promise of an untapped ability to stride confidently across the Sahara and be back in Marrakesh in time for lunch. Obviously all those people trundling around Surrey in their Range Rovers and Toyota Land Cruisers never actually use that ability – 'Yes, I'd love to forge across North Africa, darling, but we've got the Frimley-Naterjacks coming for dinner, and finding fresh langoustines is simply a nightmare' – but at least they know they could if they wanted to. So what, in the name of all that is holy, is this abomination about? A pretend 4x4 that would get stuck in a puddle and doesn't even have the saving grace of looking rugged. In fact, its appearance was less rugged than Harry Potter and served to tell the world only one thing – that, thanks to some disturbing and hitherto undocumented psychological condition, you appear to think you are Barbie.

AUSTIN ALLEGRO

This is the Godfather of the crap car. A pig-faced wretch from the days when British Leyland would have trouble making toast, never mind an entire car, the Allegro was cursed from the start. The poor bloke who designed it actually had something far sleeker and more attractive in mind, if only he hadn't made the disastrous mistake of working for a British car company in the 1970s. First the engineers insisted on fitting a ludicrously tall engine that messed up the rakish front end. Then the people who translated his original designs into actual metal got their maths wrong and made the sides all bulbous and fat. Finally, some clot from marketing insisted that it would be a corking idea to fit a square steering wheel. Short of paying someone to wait by the door of every Austin showroom and greet prospective customers with a punch in the throat, there really wasn't much more they could have done to completely scupper themselves. In fact the only bit of the Allegro they got even vaguely right was the rust-proofing. Which just meant that, unlike most BL crocks, the sodding things were annoyingly hard to kill.

VOLKSWAGEN BEETLE

The Allegro is the Godfather but this, let it be told, is
The Daddy. For some reason, beardy peacenicks and
straggly-haired surfer dudes love the Beetle, apparently
thinking it 'cool' and 'alternative'. Which is fine,
although it does rather overlook the fact that it's also
clearly 'bollocks'. What we have here is a dismal
germanic car with its engine in the wrong place
and a list of in-built faults so long that it could fill
every page in this book. Just to give you a taster,
you should know that it's slow, it's noisy, it's uncom-
fortable and it has such a completely pathetic heater
that on cold days you'd be better off setting fire to your hair.
The Beetle doesn't make you alternative and interesting at all –
it simply marks you out as the kind of mush-brained tit who knows
nothing about cars and who gives names to inanimate objects. The only
good thing about this cramped, ugly waste of perfectly good metal is that
after 57 years of continuous production – about 55 years too long –
Volkswagen finally killed it off. And good riddance.